The Amazing Animals of Australia

About the Book

The Tasmanian Devil is a terrible-looking animal. He is about as big as a large house cat, but most people say they would not like to have him for a pet! No one would ever try to make a pet out of the wild Pouched Wolf, either, or the bad-tempered Cuscus. But if you had lots of flowers, could you tame a family of Noolbengers?

William Wise's second book about amazing animals is as exciting as his first — *The Amazing Animals of Latin America*.

The Amazing Animals of Australia

by William Wise

Illustrated by Joseph Sibal

A
SEE and READ
BEGINNING TO READ
BOOK

G. P. Putnam's Sons   New York

Library of Congress Catalog Card Number: 75-90863

PRINTED IN THE UNITED STATES OF AMERICA
07209

For a long, long time very little was
known about the great island of
Australia. Hardly anyone from our own
part of the world had ever been there.

No one had seen what the country
was like.

No one knew if the days were hot or
cold.

And no one knew what amazing
animals might live in that faraway land.

Then the first Western settlers came to live in Australia.

They climbed the mountains. They crossed the deserts. They began to build houses, farms, and roads.

Little by little the settlers learned about the land. They learned that the island of Australia was a wonderful place to live. Before long, they began to tell the rest of the world what the new country was like.

Today we know a great many things about Australia.

We know about the mountains and the deserts.

We know when the days will be hot and when they will be cold.

We know about the animals, too. Some of them are very big. Some are very small.

Some live alone. Some live in large families.

We know that the animals of Australia are strange and wonderful. They are amazing animals which you cannot find in any other part of the world.

One of the strangest animals of
Australia is the Platypus. He does not
look like any animal you have ever seen.

He has a short, flat tail and very small
eyes.

His mouth is very big. It does not
look like the mouth of an animal. It
looks more like the bill of a duck. That
is why some people call him the
Duckbill Platypus.

A Platypus always lives near the water. He finds his food in lakes and rivers. He digs for his food on the bottom, in the mud.

He has four webbed feet. He can swim very well, thanks to his four webbed feet.

On each back leg the male Platypus
has a little spur. The spurs are very
sharp. They are poison spurs. Very few
animals in the world have poison spurs
which they can hurt you with.

The male Platypus does not *like* to use
his poison, though. He will use it only if
he thinks you might try to harm him.

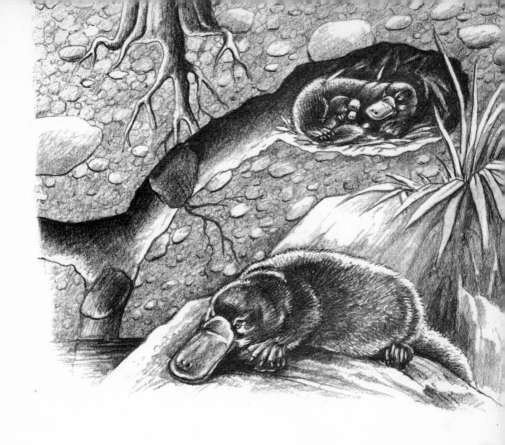

The female Platypus has no spurs and
cannot hurt you with poison. She can do
something else, though. She can lay eggs.

Birds lay eggs, of course. So do snakes.
But only two *mammals* in the world can
lay eggs — and one of them is the
female Platypus.

The only other *mammal* in the world that can lay eggs is the female Spiny Anteater.

You will find the Spiny Anteater in many parts of Australia. He is a small, strange-looking animal. He does just what his name says. He "eats ants."

The Spiny Anteater has spines all over his back. The spines are sharp. Other animals do not like to touch his sharp spines.

If a bigger animal comes near, the Spiny Anteater digs a hole in the ground. He has strong claws on his feet and can dig a hole very quickly.

When the hole is finished, the Spiny
Anteater hides in it. Only his sharp
spines stick out. The bigger animal sees
nothing but spines. He knows he can
find a better dinner somewhere else. So
he walks away and leaves the Spiny
Anteater alone.

The best-known animals of Australia
are the Kangaroos. Some of the small
Kangaroos are only about a foot long.
They look like rats.

Those that have short noses are called Short-Nosed Rat Kangaroos. Those that have long noses are called Long-Nosed Rat Kangaroos.

The Tree Kangaroo is a bigger animal.
Most of the time you will find him in a
tree. At night he even sleeps in a tree.

When the Tree Kangaroo wants to get
to the ground, he jumps down. He can
jump a long way. A Tree Kangaroo can
jump fifty feet when he wants to get to
the ground quickly.

Some Kangaroos are not even called
Kangaroos. They are called Wallabies.
One kind has a nice name. He is called
the Pretty-Faced Wallaby.

Another kind is called the Rock
Wallaby. He lives among the rocks. He
can climb and hop among the rocks and
never fall.

Some people say he lives like a
mountain goat. They say that the Rock
Wallaby *is* the mountain goat of
Australia.

One Kangaroo is called the Gray Forester. He likes to live where there are many trees. You will find him near the forests of Australia.

The Gray Forester is a big animal, but there is another Kangaroo that is even bigger.

The Great Red Kangaroo is the
biggest Kangaroo in the world. When he
sits up on his back legs and tail, he is
taller than a tall man. He does not walk.
He hops. He can hop more than twenty
feet at a time.

The Great Red Kangaroo eats only grass. He likes to live on the plains, where there is plenty of grass to eat.

Great Red Kangaroos live together in big families. Each family is called a Mob. The oldest and biggest male is the leader of the Mob. He is called a Boomer.

A mother is called a Blue Flyer.
A baby is called a Joey.

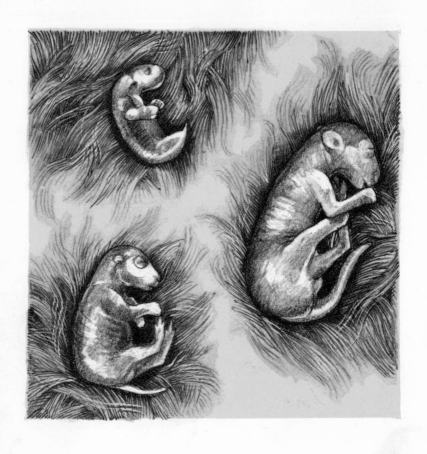

When he is born, a baby Kangaroo is very, very small. He is only about as big as your thumb.

A Joey lives for a long time inside his mother's pouch. When he grows bigger he puts his head out and looks around.

When he is bigger still, the Joey learns
how to climb out of his mother's pouch.
All day he eats grass and plays in the
warm sun.

At night the Joey climbs back inside
his mother's pouch and goes to sleep.

An animal that has a pouch is called a
Marsupial. All Kangaroos are Marsupials.
Most of the other animals in Australia
are Marsupials, too.

The Wombat is a strange-looking Marsupial. He is about the size of a big, heavy dog. He has only four front teeth. He eats grass, leaves, and other green things.

All Wombats are great diggers. They
dig tunnels more than a hundred feet
long.

At the end of the tunnel the Wombat makes a nest. He fills it with leaves. At night he goes out to eat. When day comes, you will find the Wombat back in his nest, sleeping among the leaves.

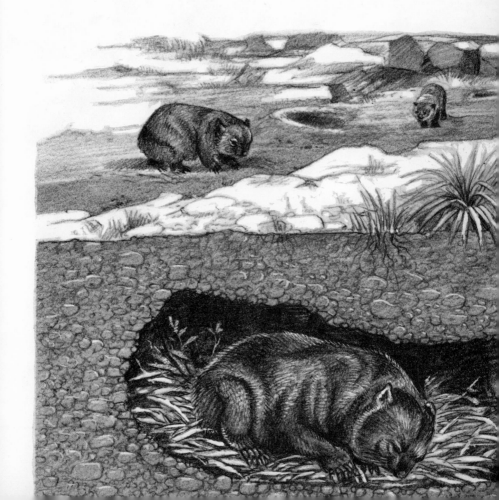

There are a number of Marsupial Cats
in Australia. One of them is about three
feet long. He is called the Common
Tiger Cat. He lives in the trees. He eats
other animals when he can catch them.

The Common Tiger Cat is much
bigger than the other Marsupial Cats of
Australia. The others are only about as
big as our own house cats.

But Marsupial Cats are not tame
animals like house cats. They are wild
animals and do not make good pets.

The Tasmanian Devil is a terrible-looking animal. He is about as big as a very big house cat. He likes to eat other animals, too.

There are those who say that he makes
a good pet if you tame him. Most
people, though, would rather have a
different animal for a pet. They say they
would not feel happy with a Tasmanian
Devil around the house.

No one would ever try to make a pet
out of the wild Pouched Wolf.
He is a much bigger animal than the
Tasmanian Devil. He looks very much
like the wolves that live in our own part
of the world.

Most of the time the Pouched Wolf walks or runs along the ground. When he wants to go very fast, he hops on his back legs like a Kangaroo.

The Pouched Wolf can open his
mouth very wide. He has dreadful teeth.
He has a dreadful bite. When he fights
with a dog, the Pouched Wolf almost
always wins.

45

You cannot always tell what an animal is like by the way he looks. The Marsupial Mole looks like a dreadful animal, but he really is not at all.

The Marsupial Mole lives in the desert, where it is hot and dry. He has no eyes. He does not have to see, though. Most of the time he lives below the ground, down in the desert sand.

Every now and then the Marsupial Mole comes up for air. He walks a little way above the ground. Then he digs a new hole for himself. Soon he goes down again, under the desert sand.

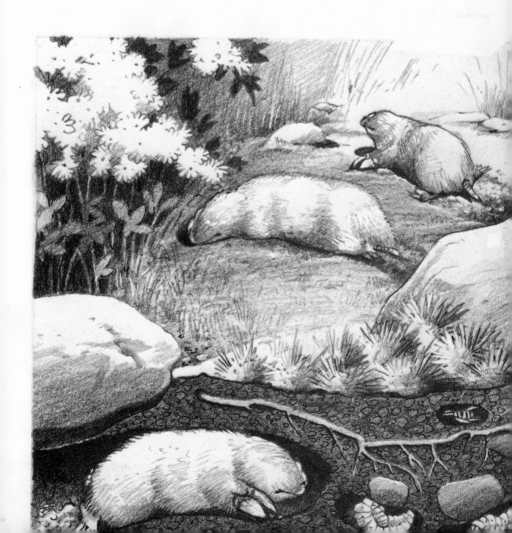

The Cuscus is a small animal that lives in the trees. He does not like to run. He does not like to jump.

He likes to walk around very slowly, high above the ground.

The Cuscus sleeps all through the day. When it grows dark, he goes out to look for his supper.

If you think the Cuscus would be in a good temper after all that sleep, you would be wrong. The Cuscus is almost *never* in a good temper. He is a slow-moving animal that likes to be left alone.

One of the most amazing animals of
Australia is the Noolbenger. There really
is no other animal like him in the world.

The Noolbenger is about as big as a small house mouse. He has a very long nose and a very long tongue for such a little animal.

The amazing Noolbenger feeds on flowers like a bee. But he does not like to eat alone. As soon as it grows dark, he comes out with his family and his friends.

Then all of the Noolbengers begin to
feed together.

They run and jump. To reach the
flowers, they sometimes hang by their
tails. They eat and eat and do not stop
until they are full.

53

The Koala is one animal that many
children will know about.

The Koala looks like a small "Teddy"
bear. He lives in the trees. He eats the
leaves of the eucalyptus tree. The leaves
of the eucalyptus tree are the only food
in the world that the Koala can eat.

One day, a long time ago, a man saw
a Koala in a tree. The man wanted to
make a new toy for children. So he made
a stuffed Koala Bear.

Before long, people everywhere saw
the new toy. They liked it so much that
they bought a "Koala Bear" for their
children.

Today children all over the world have
toy Koala Bears to play with. They look
just like the real Koala — one of the
most wonderful of all the amazing
animals in faraway Australia.

Key Words

Australia	Pouch
Claws	Settlers
Desert	Sharp
Eucalyptus tree	Spine
Female	Spur
Island	Tame
Male	Tongue
Mountain	Tunnel
Plains	Webbed
Poison	Western

The Animals

Blue Flyer

Boomer

Common Tiger Cat

Cuscus

Gray Forester

Joey

Kangaroo(s)

Koala

Mammal(s)

Marsupial (Cat,

    Mole, Kangaroo)

Noolbenger

Platypus (Duckbill)

Pouched Wolf

Spiny Anteater

Tasmanian Devil

Wallaby (Wallabies)

Wombat

The Author

William Wise is the prizewinning author of more than a dozen books for young readers. His books on exciting creatures of fact and fiction include *In the Time of the Dinosaurs, The World of Giant Mammals, Monsters of the Ancient Seas,* and *The Amazing Animals of Latin America.* Among his many books for older children are *The Two Reigns of Tutankhamen,* which received a Boys' Clubs of America Junior Book Award Medal, and *Alexander Hamilton,* a Junior Literary Guild Selection.

The Artist

Joseph Sibal is a natural history artist whose paintings
have illustrated semitechnical publications issued by mu-
seums. His paintings have also been reproduced in popu-
lar magazines, such as *Life*. For Putnam's, Mr. Sibal
has also illustrated *Monsters of the Ancient Seas, The
Strange World of Dinosaurs, The Strange World of
Reptiles, The Strange World of Insects,* and *The Amazing Animals of Latin America.*